MODULAR ORIGAMI POLYHEDRA

Revised and Enlarged Edition

Lewis Simon, Bennett Arnstein, and Rona Gurkewitz

DOVER PUBLICATIONS, INC.
Mineola, New York

Dedication

This book is dedicated to the memories of Karan Hall and Lewis Simon.

Acknowledgments

The authors thank Joe Hamamoto for his model of the pentagonal dipyramid used in the picture on p. iv. We also thank Western Connecticut State University for the use of their computers and software to prepare the book. In particular, the Student Technology Training Center, Journalism Lab, Graphic Arts Lab, and Math and Computer Science Department provided their support. Special thanks go to M. C. Waldrep, Managing Editor at Dover Publications, for her thoughtful advice and apt assistance with preparation of the text and graphics files, and to Doug Planker and Maddie Wolke for generously sharing their software and design expertise. Photographs were taken by Bill Quinnell.

About the Authors

Lewis Simon was a postal worker and a math teacher. He died in November 1997. Bennett Arnstein is a retired mechanical engineer who worked in the aerospace industry. Rona Gurkewitz is a math and computer science professor at Western Connecticut State University.

Copyright

Bibliographical Note

This Dover edition, first published in 1999, is a revised and enlarged republication of the work originally published in 1989 by Bennett Arnstein of Los Angeles, Calif. This edition includes some material previously published in 1995 by Dover Publications, Inc., in *3-D Geometric Origami: Modular Polyhedra*, by Rona Gurkewitz and Bennett Arnstein.

Library of Congress Cataloging-in-Publication Data

Simon, Lewis.
    Modular origami polyhedra / Lewis Simon, Bennett Arnstein, and Rona Gurkewitz. —
Rev. and enl. ed.
        p.   cm.

    1. Origami. 2. Polyhedra—Models. I. Arnstein, Bennett. II. Gurkewitz, Rona.
III. Title.
TT870.G87   1999
736'.982—dc21

99-11934
CIP

International Standard Book Number
ISBN-13: 978-0-486-40476-9
ISBN-10: 0-486-40476-5

Manufactured in the United States by Courier Corporation
40476507   2014
www.doverpublications.com

Contents

Clockwise: 12-Module Decoration Box from 2x1s adapted from dollar bills
30-Module Dodecahedron from 108-degree module from 4x3s
12-Module Decoration Box from 2x1s
15-Module Pentagonal Dipyramid from 60-degree half-square Plank modules

Part 1
Introduction

Clockwise from upper right: 24-Module Cuboctahedron from 90- to 60-degree half-square Plank modules
6-Module Tetrahedron from 60-degree half-square Plank modules
12-Module Octahedron from 60-degree half-square Plank modules
30-Module Icosahedron from 60-degree half-square Plank modules

Introduction

As the title indicates, this book is a revised and enlarged edition of the original *Modular Origami Polyhedra,* by Lewis Simon and Bennett Arnstein, which was published by Bennett Arnstein in 1989. The models included here have been developed by the authors during the course of four decades. Lewis Simon was a pioneer in the field of modular origami in the 1960s. Since that time, many people have learned to enjoy the branch of origami called modular or unit origami. This type of origami consists of making models from several pieces of paper folded in the same way. Folding the modules can be simple. It is assembly that takes some practice if you are new to this type of folding. Even assembly may not be difficult until the last piece or two must be added to the model. With practice, the assembly process becomes very clear and dexterity develops. The results make the effort worthwhile.

This book contains diagrams for constructing modules that can be used to build polyhedral shapes. It is divided into sections for three main "systems" and a section for miscellaneous modules. As in the earlier book *3-D Geometric Origami: Modular Polyhedra* (by Gurkewitz and Arnstein), we define a "system" of models as a collection of models that can be folded from different numbers of a given module or from modules that have related folding sequences. Another possibility is to vary the starting polygonal shape or the first few folds of the paper used for a module. A third possibility is to systematically vary an angle or angles on a module to produce a new module that makes a different polyhedron.

The Sonobe system, named after Mitsunobu Sonobe of Japan, is comprised of models made from different numbers of the basic module, creased in different ways, as well as a module with properties related to those of the basic module. The basic module can be viewed as a chain of four right triangles. The Sonobe polyhedral shapes made from the basic module are distinctive because their faces are all 45-45-90 right triangles or a combination of several such triangles. This book includes some foldings of the basic module designed by Lewis Simon, namely the 12-module cube and the 24-module cube. New in this book is the integration of the Sonobe shapes into the Decoration Box system. The generalization of the basic Sonobe module from a chain of four 45-45-90 right triangles to a chain of four equilateral triangles is different from the two similarly functioning modules in *3-D Geometric Origami.* Other foldings of the basic module are possible and have been explored by Tomoko Fuse and Michael Naughton.

We think that Lewis Simon was one of the first to fold a stellated octahedron from Sonobe modules. We have included the stellated octahedron and the stellated icosahedron as models in this book. It should be noted that the stellation process has been generalized by Kasahara and others to building polyhedra with 3-, 4-, 5-, 6-, or 8-sided faces. To do this one builds a compound of pyramids for each polygon that is a face of the polyhedron. The number of pyramids in the compound will be based on the number of sides of the polygon. This book illustrates how to join three modules together to make a cube-corner pyramid. For 3-, 4-, 5-, and 6-sided faces of the polyhedron, the same number of pyramids are joined at a vertex to make a compound. For an 8-sided face, an octagonal compound is made up of four 3-sided compounds and five 4-sided compounds. There is a central 4-sided compound surrounded by alternating 3- and 4-sided compounds.

The Decoration Box, by Lewis Simon, and the 108-Degree-Module Dodecahedron designed by Lewis Simon (and independently by Bob Neale) date to the 1960s. Development of this system continues to this day and takes many interesting forms. Included in the book are improvements and modifications developed by Bennett Arnstein; adaptation to money folding as well as various modifications by Rona Gurkewitz; and ideas on using 4x3 paper and different angles, contributed by Jim Plank. Jim Plank has a Web site devoted to polyhedra that can be made using variations of the Decoration Box system. This book shows how to construct the cube-corner stellated Sonobe shapes as well as polyhedra with faces that consist of 45-, 60-, 90-, or 108-degree angles.

The Gyroscope by Lewis Simon is so named because it twirls around like a gyroscope when held between two fingers and blown upon. It has been generalized to a triangle and "sunkated" (the module's point is "sunk," which results in truncation of the polyhedron built with it). Some advice on how to mass-produce equilateral triangles is included in this book. Many models can be made from the modules shown. Also, one-piece versions of the square and triangular Gyroscope and a pentagonal version appear in *3-D Geometric Origami* by Gurkewitz and Arnstein.

60-Module Cube-Corner Stellated Icosahedron from 2x1s
(a Sonobe shape from Decoration Box modules with a 90-degree angle
on one end and a 45-degree angle on the other)

Part 2
Preliminaries

Clockwise: Modular Cube (p. 29)
Decoration Box with Reverse-Side Color Exposed (p. 24)
Modular Cube (p. 36)
Modular Cube (p. 26)

Polyhedral Basis for Models in Book

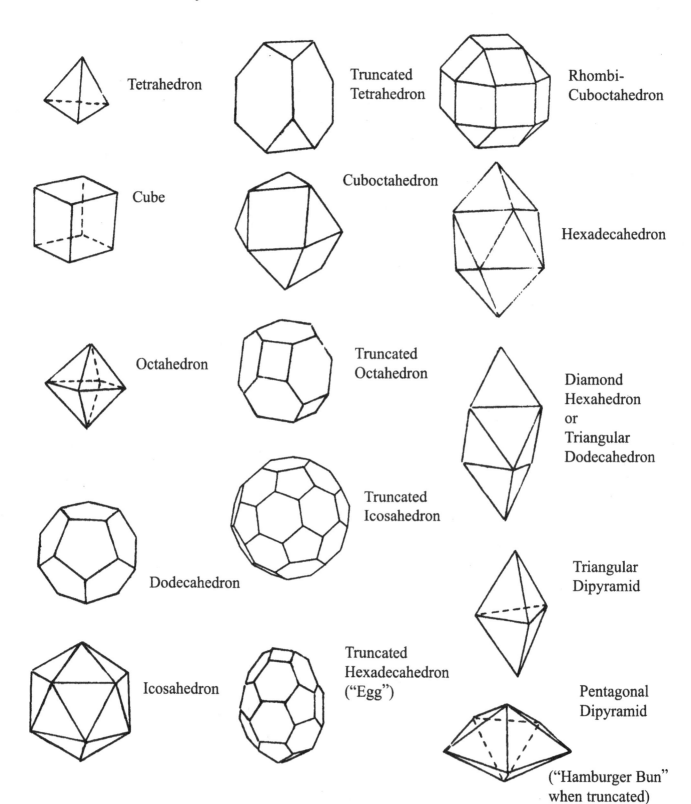

Tetrahedron

Truncated Tetrahedron

Rhombi-Cuboctahedron

Cube

Cuboctahedron

Hexadecahedron

Octahedron

Truncated Octahedron

Diamond Hexahedron or Triangular Dodecahedron

Dodecahedron

Truncated Icosahedron

Triangular Dipyramid

Icosahedron

Truncated Hexadecahedron ("Egg")

Pentagonal Dipyramid

("Hamburger Bun" when truncated)

Assembly Instructions

General: In most cases it is best to start assembling and then add modules one at a time. Exceptions to this rule are noted below.

Sonobe System: There are many, many possible shapes to be made from the basic module. We have hardly scratched the surface in this book. See the introduction for a description of how to make additional polyhedra. Also, vary the folds on the module from mountain to valley to get different shapes. When making 6-module cubes. note that modules next to each other have their long creases perpendicular to each other. The corners of a 12-module cube are self-locking, so when you are making one you always must complete a corner that has been started before proceeding elsewhere. Linear extensions of these cubes can be made, but require glue except at the cubes' corners.

Decoration Box System: Each module will link up with four other modules: two into which it is inserted and two that are inserted into it. The angles of the modules may vary and so result in different polyhedra. Using a different angle at each end of a module results in still more polyhedra. 12-module cubes are shapes based on the 12-module Sonobe cubes. When the 108-degree module is used to make a dodecahedron, a completed corner is self-locking, so always finish a started corner before proceeding elsewhere.

Gyroscope System: For the square-based Gyroscope, arranging three modules to make a cube corner and then adding on to it works best. For the triangle-based Gyroscope, subassemblies consisting of rings of three, four, or five triangular gyroscope modules can be made when building a truncation of a shape with triangular faces. These subassemblies may be considered to be supermodules. Three supermodules form a 6-sided ring around the space that they surround. For additional assembly instructions for the triangle-based Gyroscope, see p. 50.

Symbols

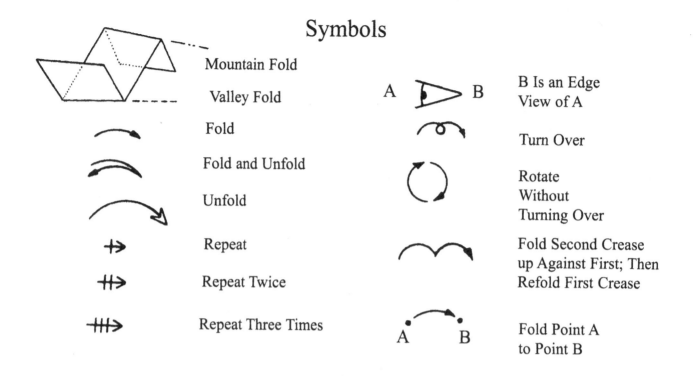

Mountain Fold

Valley Fold

Fold

Fold and Unfold

Unfold

Repeat

Repeat Twice

Repeat Three Times

B Is an Edge
View of A

Turn Over

Rotate
Without
Turning Over

Fold Second Crease
up Against First; Then
Refold First Crease

Fold Point A
to Point B

Thirds Construction

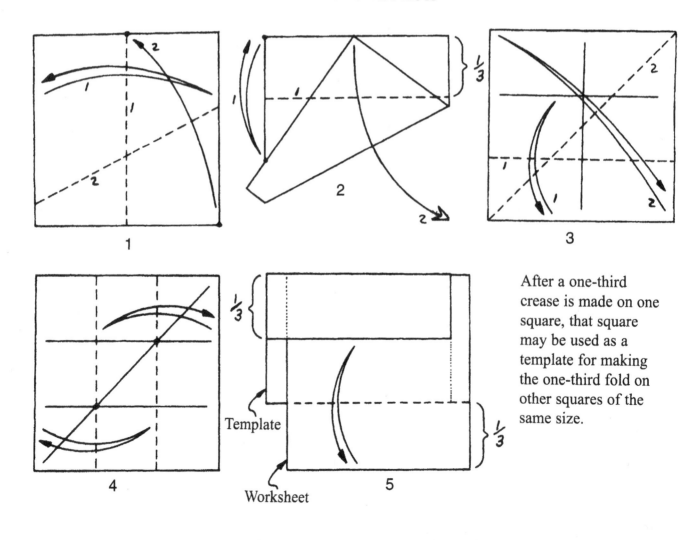

1

2

3

4

Template

Worksheet

5

After a one-third
crease is made on one
square, that square
may be used as a
template for making
the one-third fold on
other squares of the
same size.

How to Make Equilateral Triangles
by Bennett Arnstein

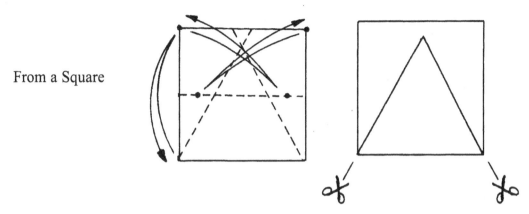

From a Square

From a Rectangle

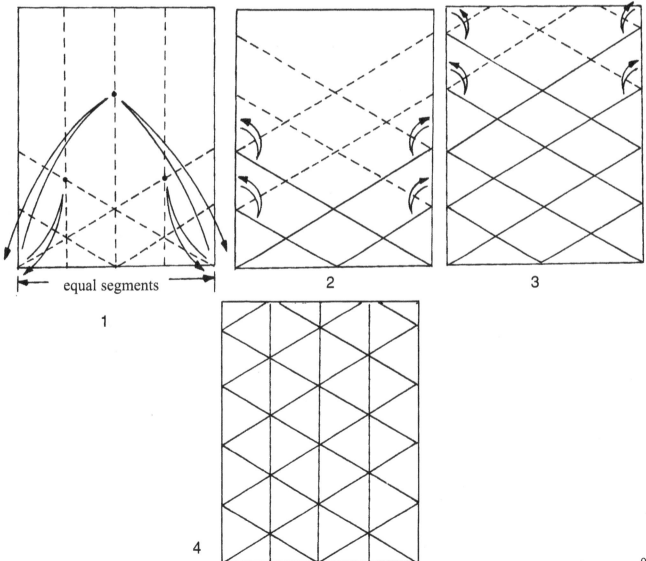

equal segments

1

2

3

4

How to Make a 2 x 1 (Half-Square) From a Dollar Bill

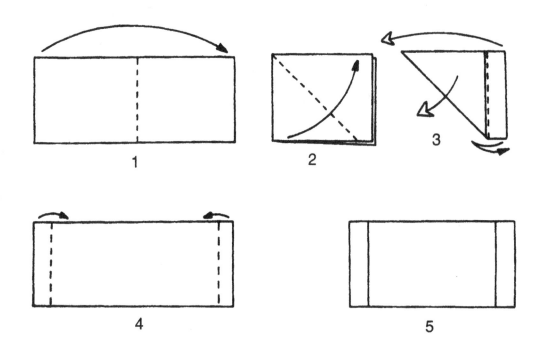

How to Make a 4 x 3 From a Dollar Bill

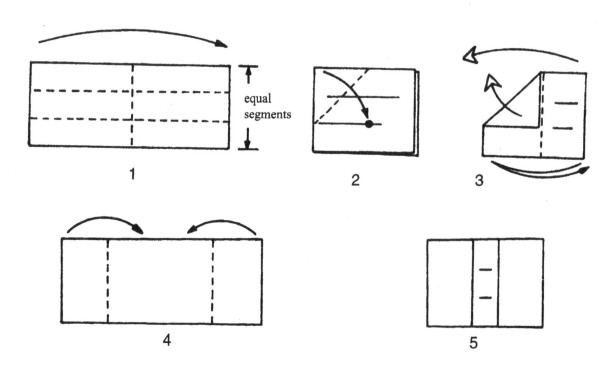

How to Make a 4 x 3 From a Square

Fold the square into four equal segments horizontally and vertically. Cut off one row of equal segments, either horizontally or vertically. You are left with a paper of 4 x 3 units.

Part 3
Sonobe System

Clockwise: 24-Module Cube
12-Module Cube
6-Module Cube
3-Module Toshie's Jewel
12-Module Stellated Octahedron
30-Module Stellated Icosahedron

Basic Sonobe Module
Chain of Four Isosceles Right Triangles Module

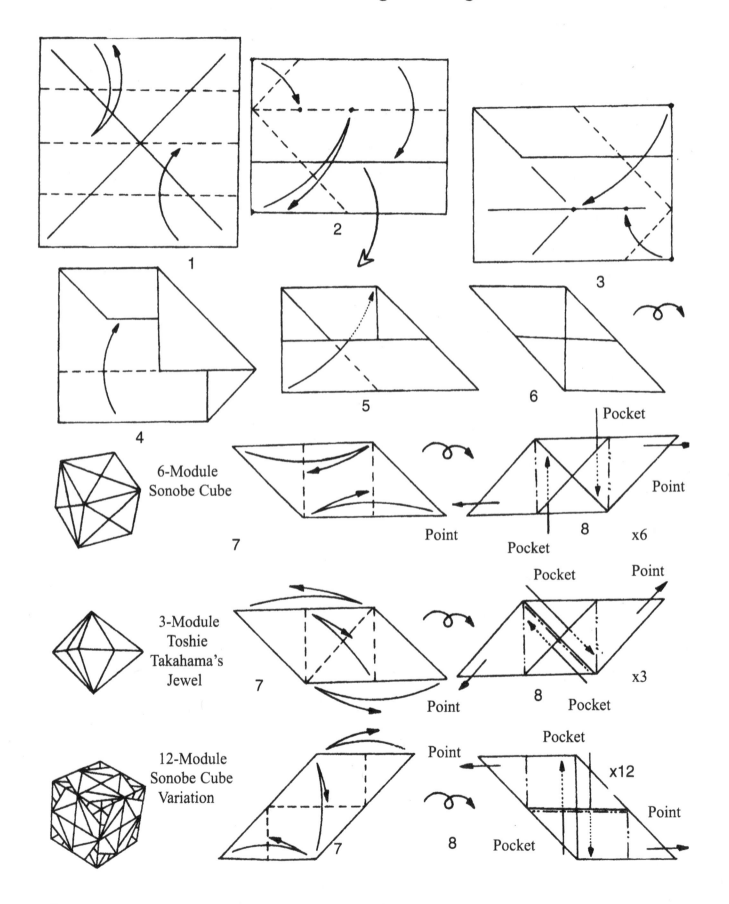

1

2

3

4

5

6

Pocket

Point

Point

Pocket

8

x6

6-Module
Sonobe Cube

7

3-Module
Toshie
Takahama's
Jewel

Pocket

Point

7

Point

8

Pocket

x3

12-Module
Sonobe Cube
Variation

Pocket

Point

7

8

Pocket

Point

x12

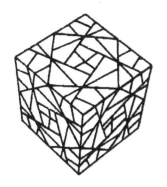

More Uses of Basic Sonobe Unit

24-Module
Sonobe Cube
Variation
(p. 14)

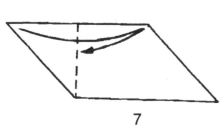

Pocket

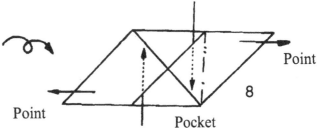

Point

Point

Point

8

Pocket

Pocket

7

12-Module
Stellated
Octahedron

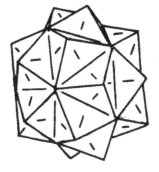

30-Module
Stellated
Icosahedron

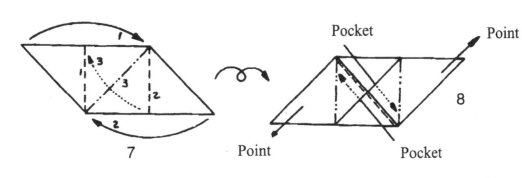

Pocket

Point

7

Point

Point

Pocket

8

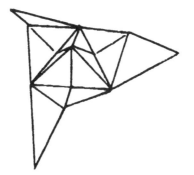

Sonobe Variation 1
by Bennett Arnstein

This is a variation of the Basic Sonobe Module. It can be folded in any of the ways the basic module can. Pictured here is the 24-module cube.

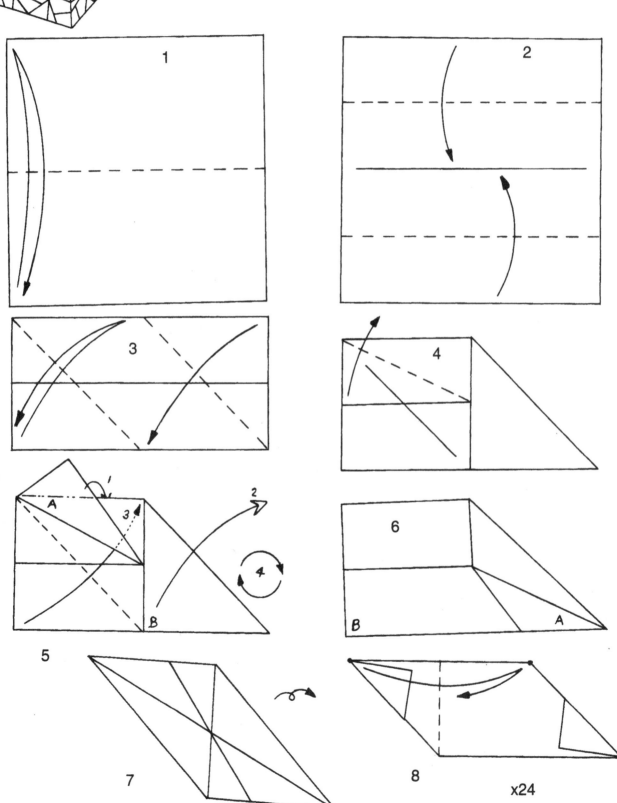

x24

Sonobe Variation 2

by Bennett Arnstein

This is a variation of the Basic Sonobe Module. It can
be folded in any of the ways the basic module can.

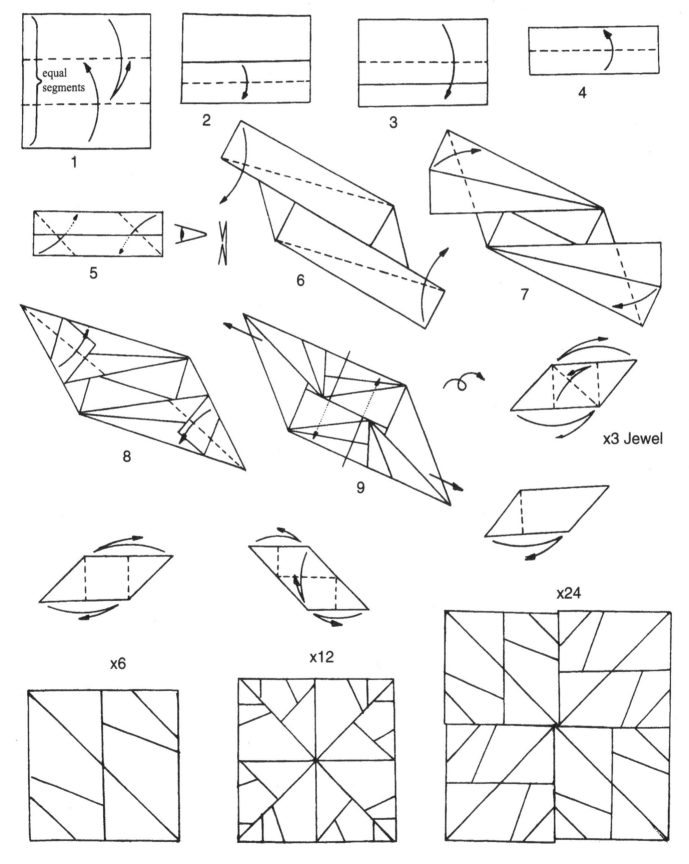

Sonobe Variation 3

by Bennett Arnstein

This is a variation of the Basic Sonobe Module. It can be folded in any of the ways the basic module can. Steps 1–7 are Lewis Simon's Pony Base. Step 8 adapts this base to the Sonobe system.

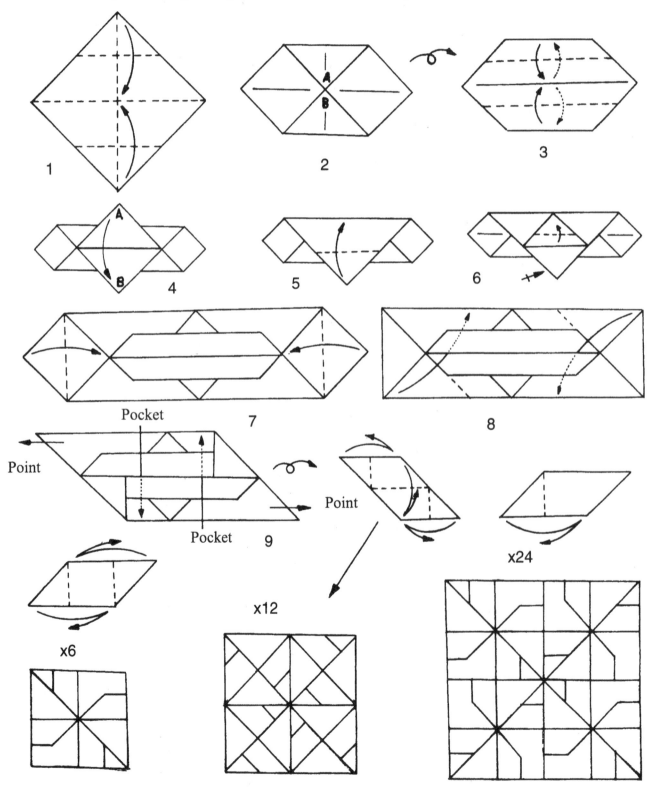

Sonobe Variation 4

by Bennett Arnstein

This is a variation of the Basic Sonobe Module. It can
be folded in any of the ways the basic module can.

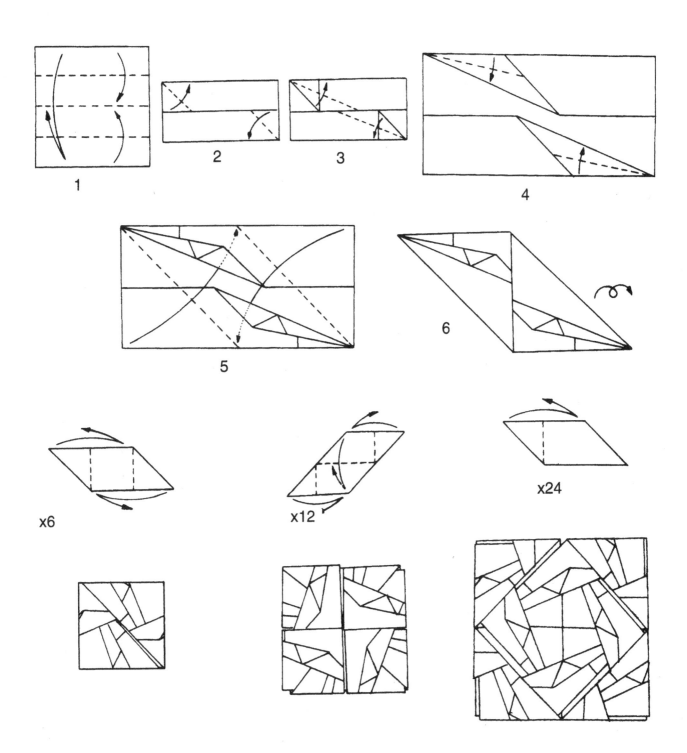

Sonobe Variation 5

by Bennett Arnstein

This is a variation of the Basic Sonobe Module. It can be folded in any of the ways the basic module can.

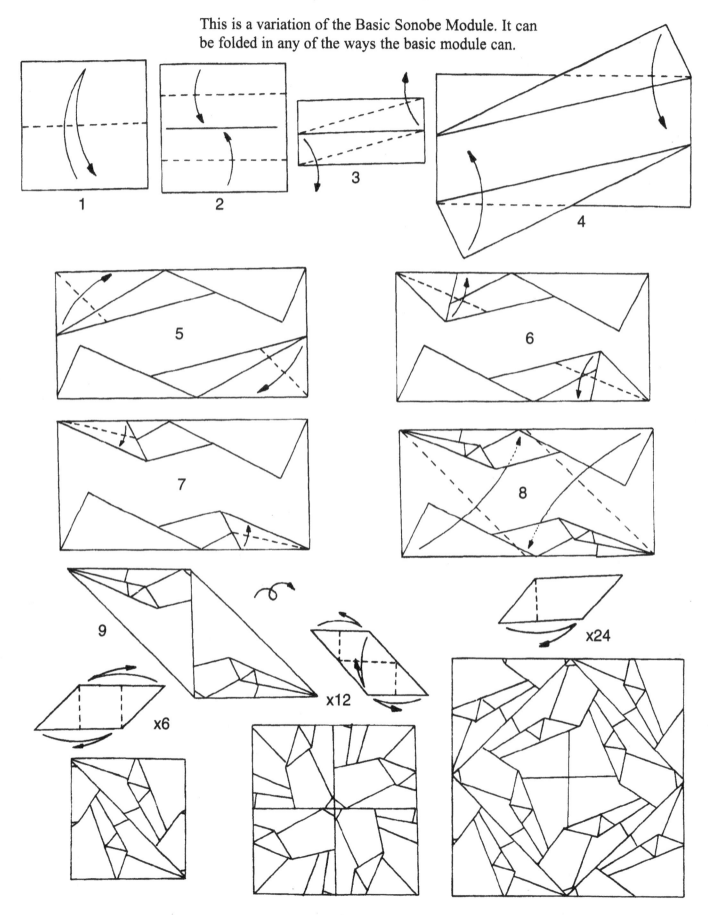

Sonobe Variation 6

by Bennett Arnstein

This is a variation of the Basic Sonobe Module. It can be folded in any of the ways the basic module can.

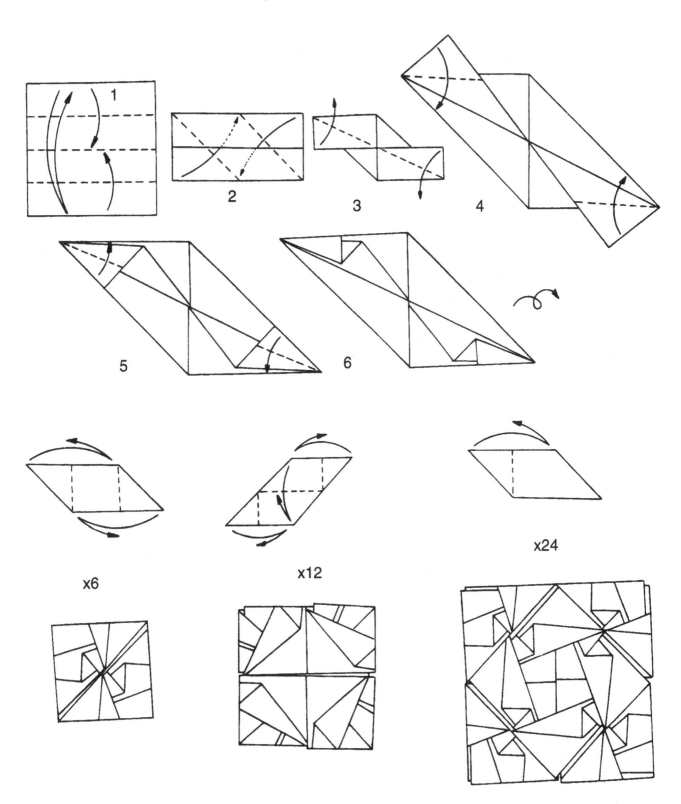

Sonobe Variation 7
by Bennett Arnstein

This is a variation of the Basic Sonobe Module. It can
be folded in any of the ways the basic module can.

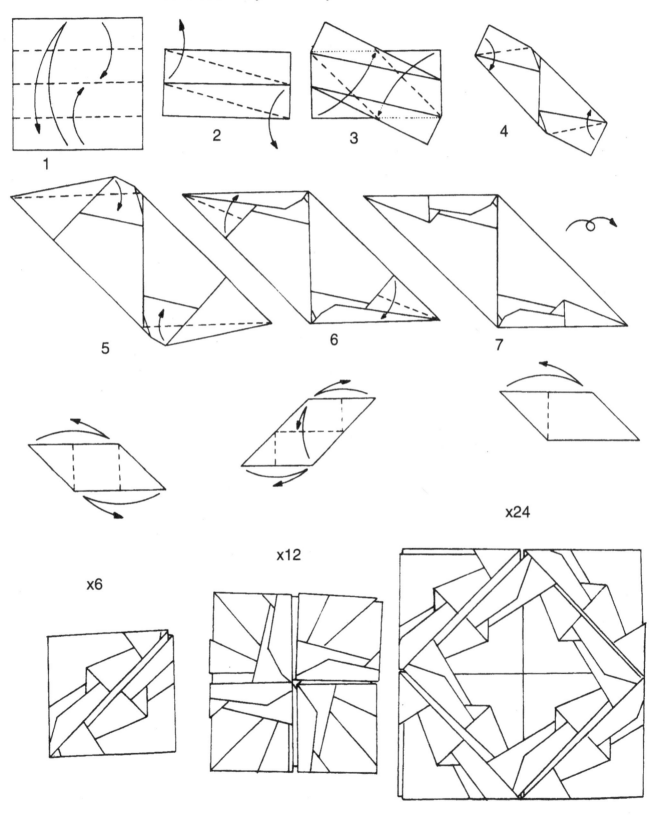

Sonobe Variation 8

by Bennett Arnstein

This is a variation of the Basic Sonobe Module. It can be folded the same way as the basic module.

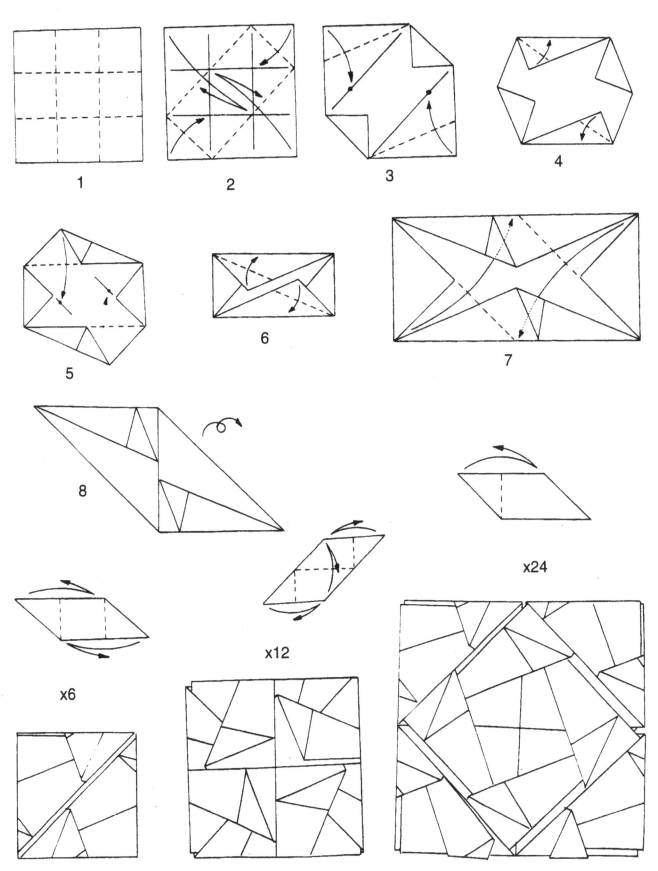

1

2

3

4

5

6

7

8

x24

x12

x6

Chain of Four Equilateral Triangles Module
by Lewis Simon and Bennett Arnstein

As drawn, this module makes stellated models. If the valley fold in step 9 is changed to a mountain fold, this module makes polyhedra with equilateral-triangle faces, such as the tetrahedron, octahedron, and icosahedron, as well as the hexadecahedron. For the icosahedron you will need 10 modules, 5 right-handed and 5 left-handed. The hexadecahedron is made from 4 right modules and 4 left modules.

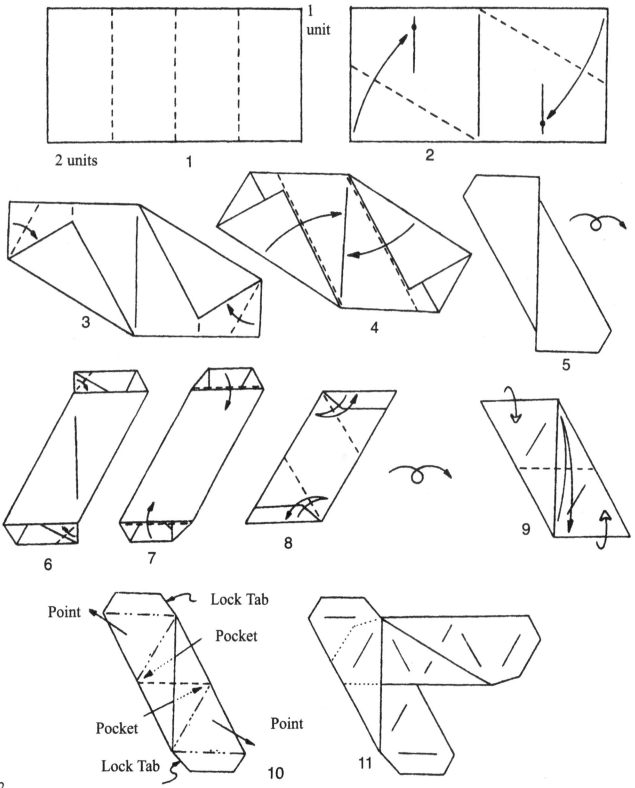

22

Part 4
Decoration Box System

Clockwise: 60-Module Stellated Icosahedron from Modified Ninja Star modules
24-Module Stellated Octahedron from Modified Ninja Star modules
12-Module Ninja Star Cube

Decoration Box

by Lewis Simon

This is the original Decoration Box. There are two 90-degree angles between the mountain creases in step 12. Variations can be made from a 2x1 half-square (p. 25), dollar bills adapted to 2x1 (p. 10), and 4x3s. Photos pp. iv and 5.

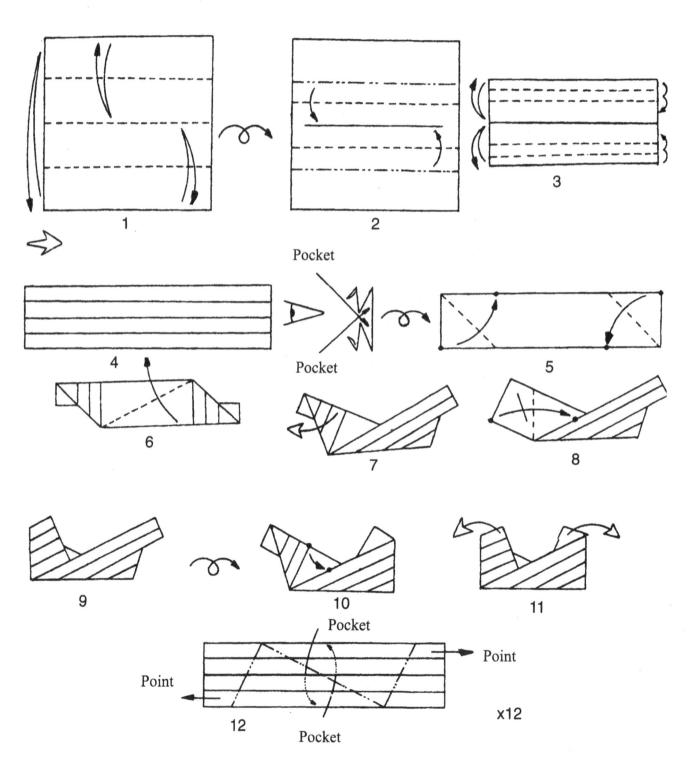

Modular Cube

by Bennett Arnstein

Variation of Lewis Simon's Decoration Box (p. 24)
LSDB #1

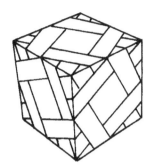

This is a simplified, lighter weight, lower cost variation of Lewis Simon's Decoration Box. It is made from 12 half-squares (2x1s), so it contains only half as much paper as the original. Starting from a 2x1 makes it possible to fold the model from dollar bills. See photo p. iv. Three modules meet at each corner of the cube. Four modules form each face of the cube.

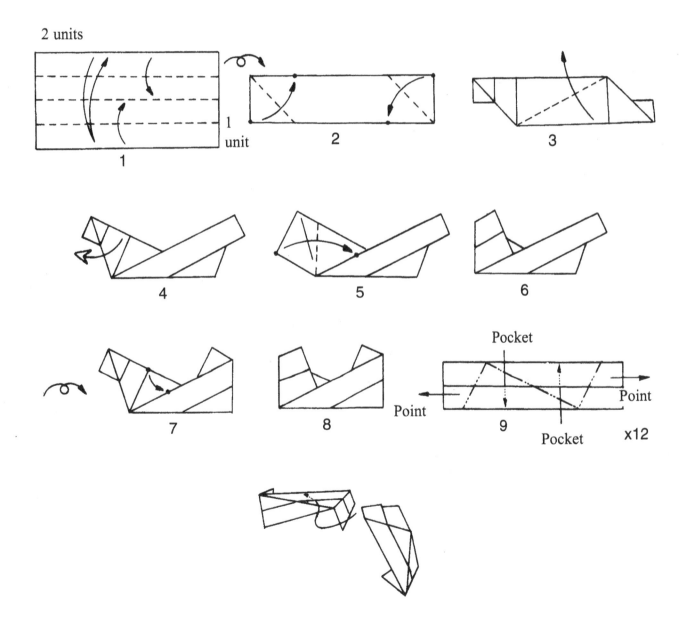

2 units

1

1 unit

2

3

4

5

6

7

8

Pocket

Point

9

Point

Pocket

x12

Modular Cube

by Bennett Arnstein

Variation of Lewis Simon's "Decoration Box"
LSDB Variation #2

This variation contains only half as much paper as the original, but also exposes the reverse-side color of the paper. Turn over step 2 and follow steps 2–8 of LSDB #1 on p. 25. When origami paper that is white on one side and colored on the other is used, contrasting colors can be displayed by using two pieces of paper back-to-back with the color on the outside, when folding a module.

2 units

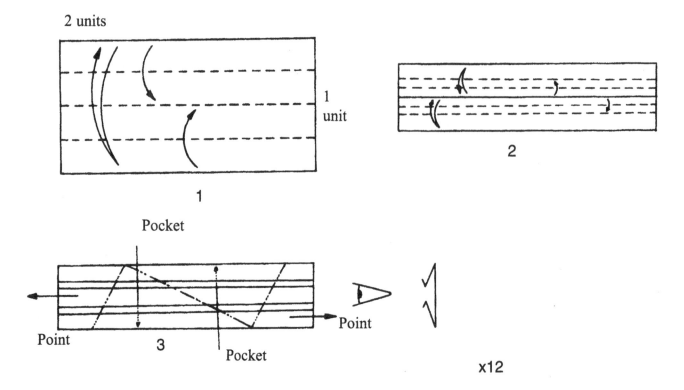

1

1
unit

2

Pocket

Point

Point

3

Pocket

Point

x12

Modular Cube:
Sonobe Cube from Decoration Box Module

by Lewis Simon

Start with step 4 of the Decoration Box
(p. 24). Twelve modules make a cube.

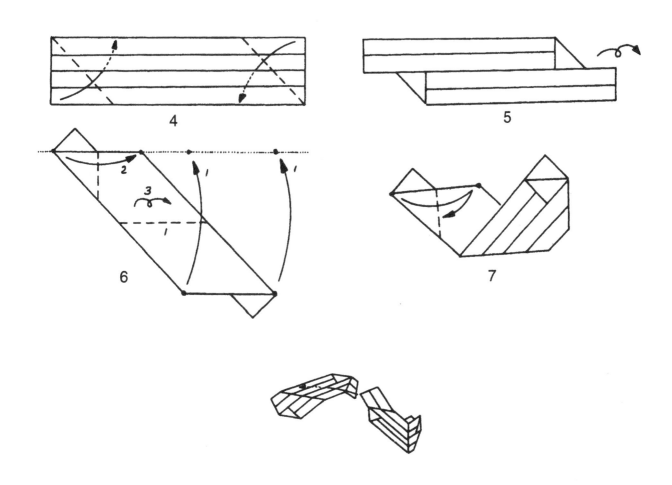

4

5

6

7

Modular Cube

by Lewis Simon

This cube is sturdier and has a more interesting
reverse-side color pattern than the cube on p. 27.
The truncated corners and square holes in the faces
are the same size. The assembly is the same as that on
p. 27.

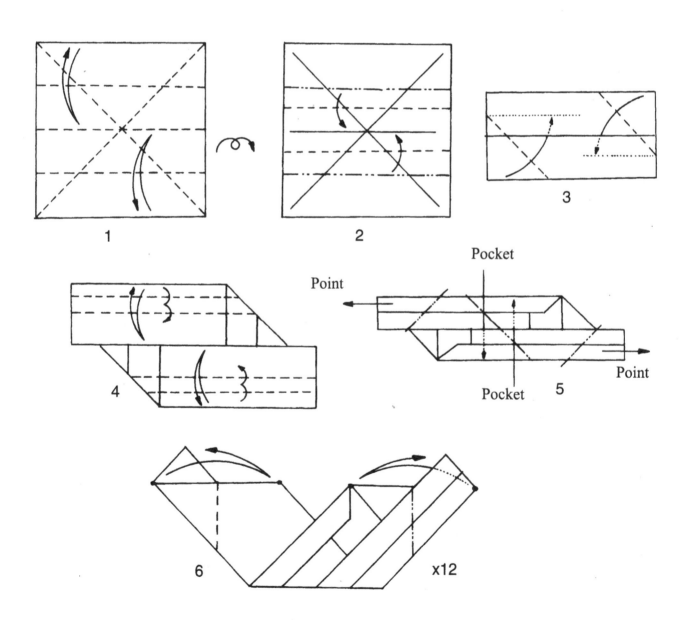

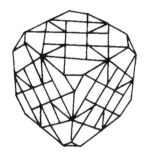

Modular Cube
by Lewis Simon

Start with step 4 of the cube on p. 28. The creases made in
step 6 are shown opened flat in step 7. This cube is sturdy
and has an interesting reverse-side color pattern. Assemble
as on p. 27.

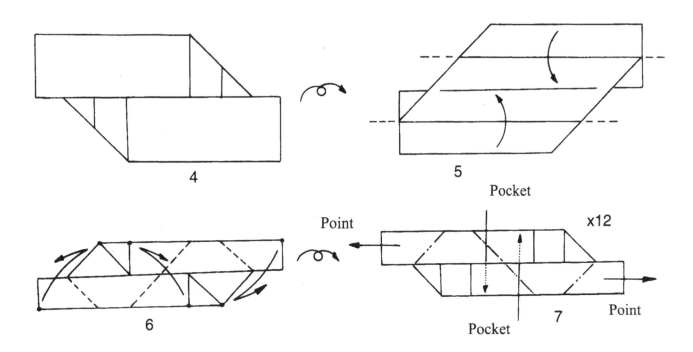

4

5

Pocket

Point

6

7

x12

Pocket

Point

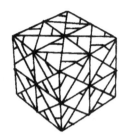

Modular Cube

by Lewis Simon

This cube is a variation of both the Decoration Box and the Sonobe 12-module cube. For assembly see p. 27.

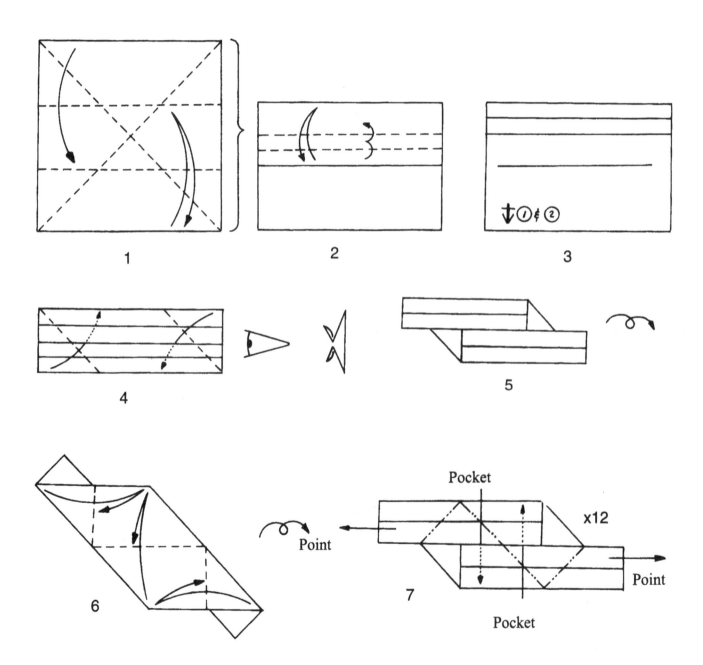

Modular Cube
by Lewis Simon

To assemble two modules as shown, the short crease on the entering module lines up with the long crease on the receiving module. Each of the twelve modules corresponds to an edge of the cube.

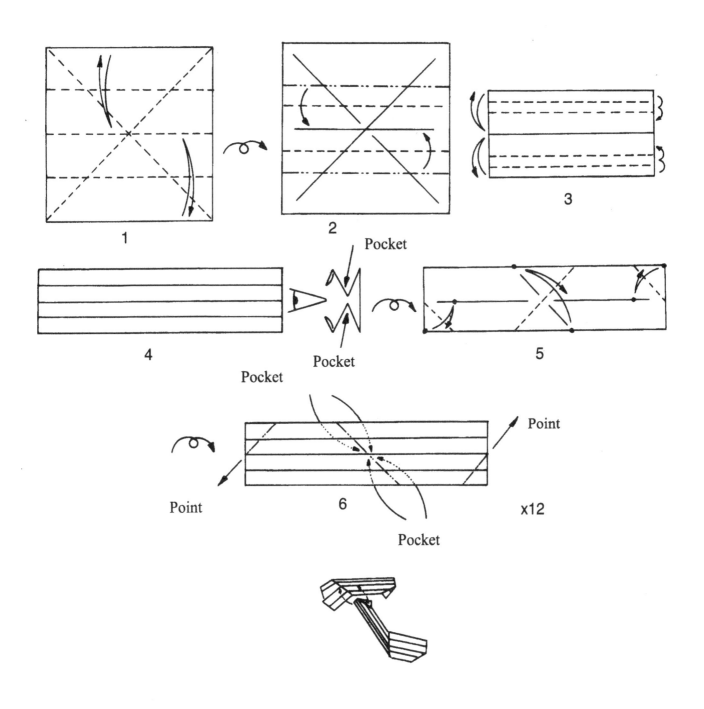

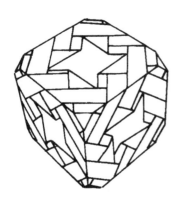

Ninja Star Cube
by Lewis Simon

This is a variation of the original Ninja Star Cube,
which has been published around the world.

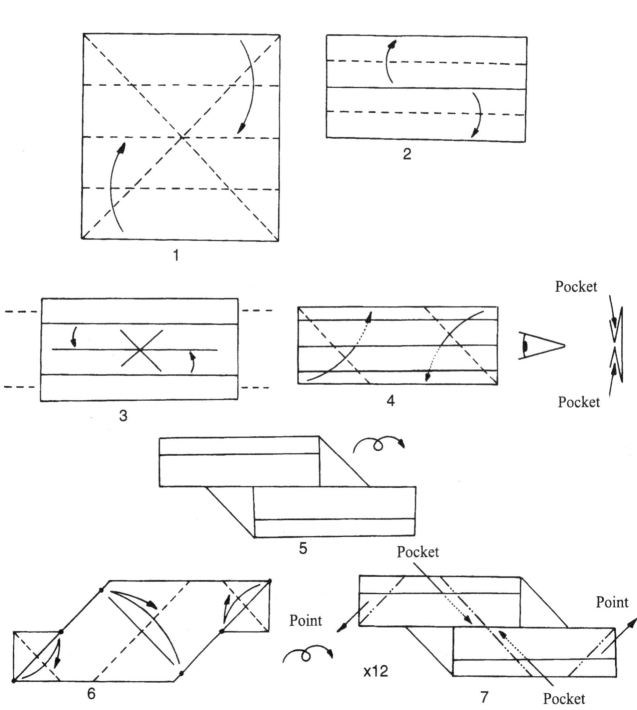

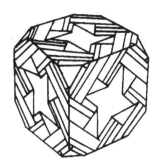

Ninja Star Cube #2
by Lewis Simon

The cube on this page is an early version of the Ninja Star Cube. In step 1, the paper is divided into three equal segments horizontally. In step 4, repeat #2 of step 1, plus step 2 and 3, on the bottom third.

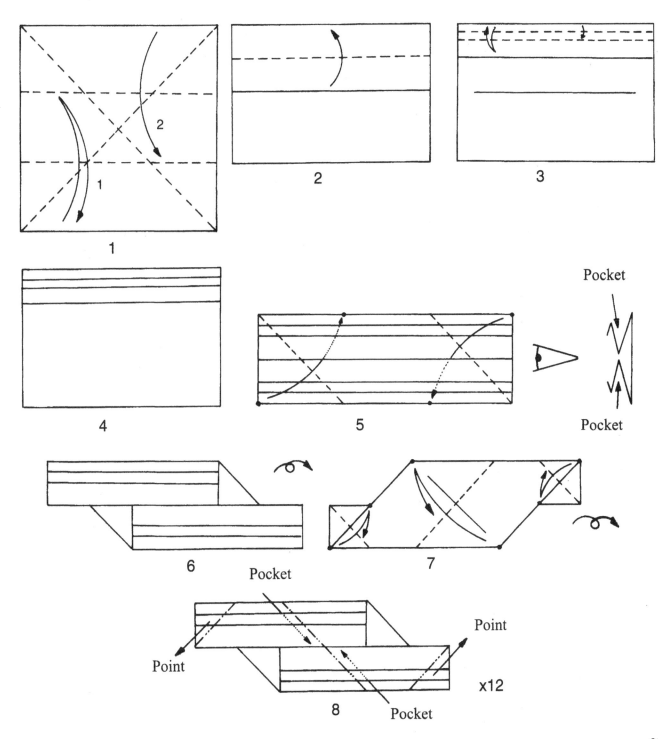

Modular Decorative Cube

by Lewis Simon and Bennett Arnstein

The first folded sheet can be used as a template to form both 3/32 cuffs on the other eleven sheets. Then you can skip from step 1 to step 7.

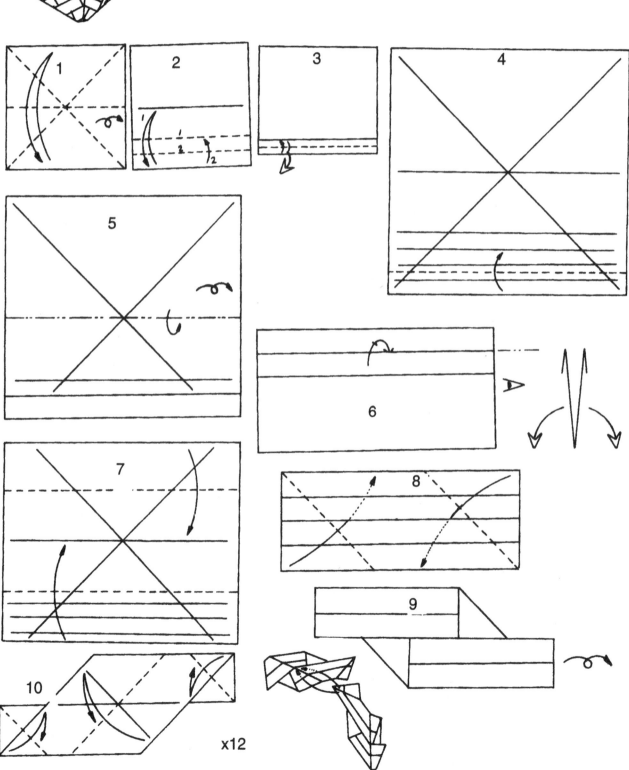

x12

Decorative Cube
by Lewis Simon

This cube can be considered a variation of the Ninja Star Cube in which the points of the Ninja Star holes have vanished, leaving a square hole in each face. A band of reverse-side color surrounds each corner. Since the original piece of paper has proportions 2:3 and is folded into three equal parts in the long direction, the easiest way to make the modules is to make a square folded into three equal parts in both directions and then cut off one third. An alternative that doesn't waste paper is to fold a square into sixths vertically and thirds horizontally, making six modules from one square, with each module being 1/3 by 3/6—that is, 2/6 x 3/6 or 2 x 3.

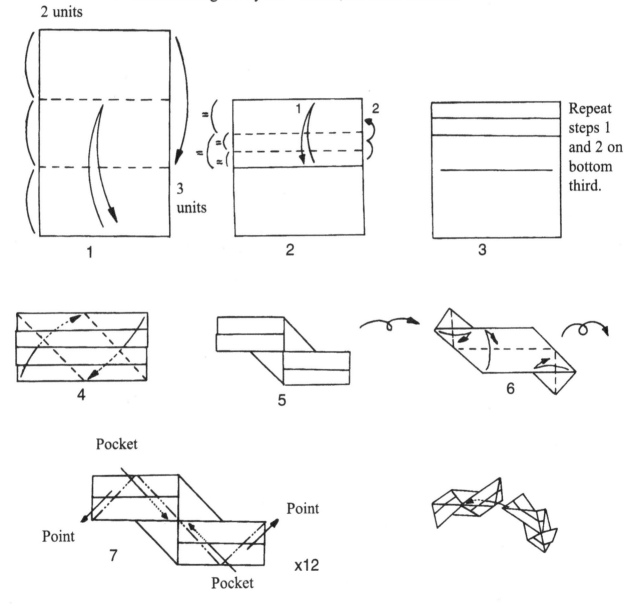

2 units

3 units

1

2

Repeat steps 1 and 2 on bottom third.

3

4

5

6

Pocket

Point

Point

7

Pocket

x12

Modular Cube
by Bennett Arnstein

This cube is the result of trying to see how closely I could duplicate
Lewis Simon's cube on p. 35 (which is made from twelve rectangles),
using twelve squares. The bands of reverse-side color on this cube form
a chain of six linked squares rotated 45 degrees to the edges of the
cube. The folding starts with step 9 on p. 34. In step 12, open each
crease to 90 degrees and assemble the modules like those on p. 35.

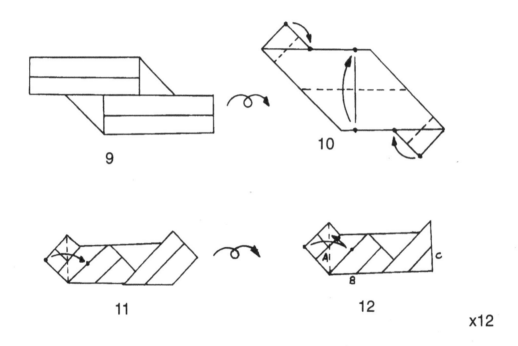

x12

Modular Cube

by Lewis Simon

Each module has two small triangles of the reverse color surrounded by the primary color. The same two colors may be used on all twelve modules or a different color combination may be used on each module. In step 1, start with the reverse side or white side up. To assemble, open the creases to 90 degrees. The short crease on the entering module lines up with the long crease on the receiving module. Three modules meet at each corner of the cube. Four modules form each face of the cube.

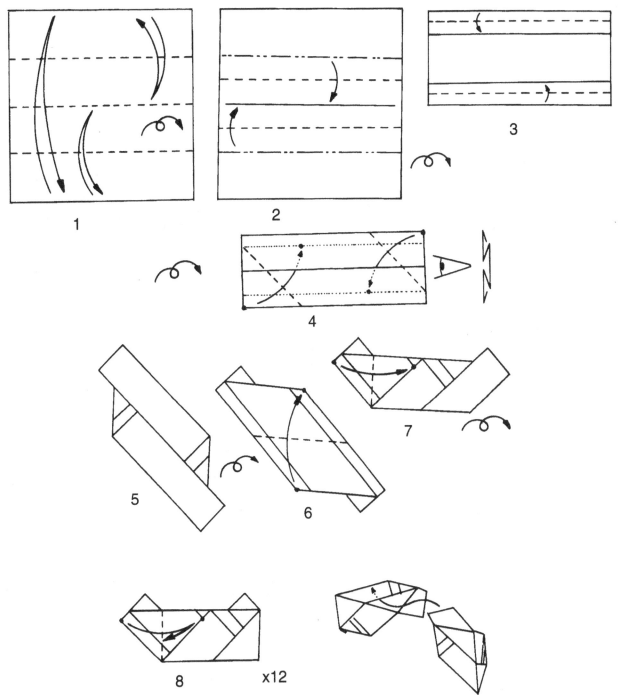

Modular Cube
by Lewis Simon

The valley crease in step 6 is the reverse side of the mountain crease made in step 1. To assemble, open the creases to 90 degrees. The short crease on the entering module lines up with the long crease on the receiving module.

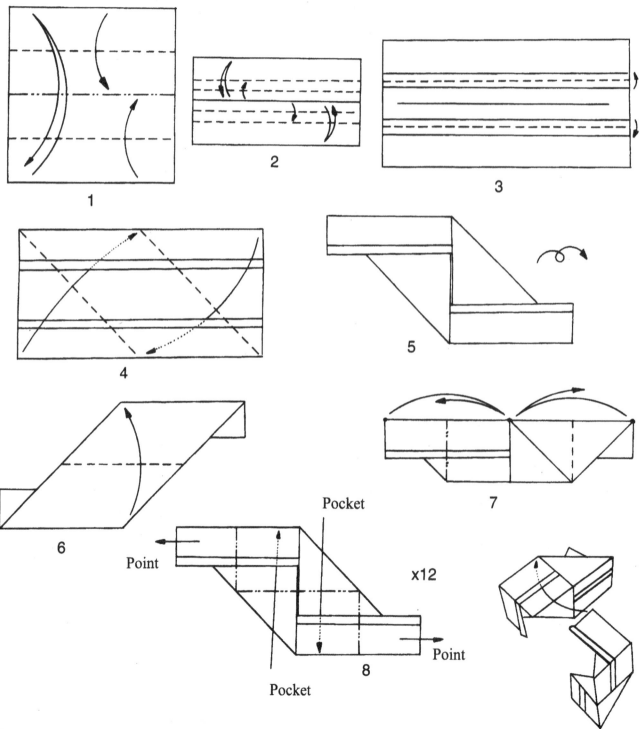

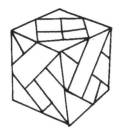

Modular Cube
by Lewis Simon

This cube is different from other 12-module cubes. For one thing, the three creases are all the same length. Also, each module has two different pockets into which the point of the adjacent module may be inserted. Moreover, if a module is reversed end-for-end, the color pattern of the cube is affected. Thus many different color patterns are possible. Figure D shows a module entering the primary pocket of the receiving module. Figure E shows a module entering the alternate pocket of the receiving module. This cube is the most difficult to assemble of those in this book.

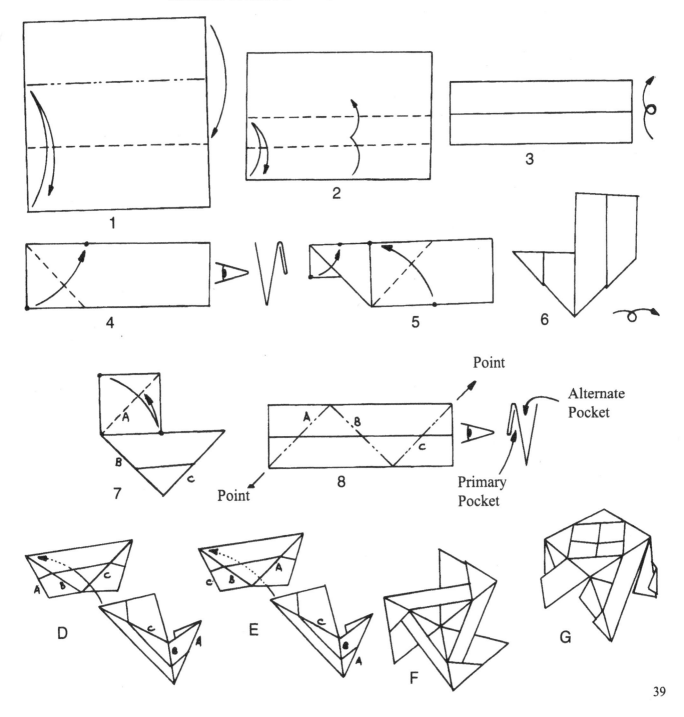

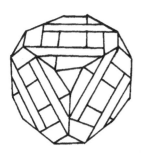

Modular Cube

by Bennett Arnstein

Variation of a cube by Lewis Simon

This cube is made from twelve half-squares, thus using only half as much paper as the original on p. 39, and is easily adapted to money folding.

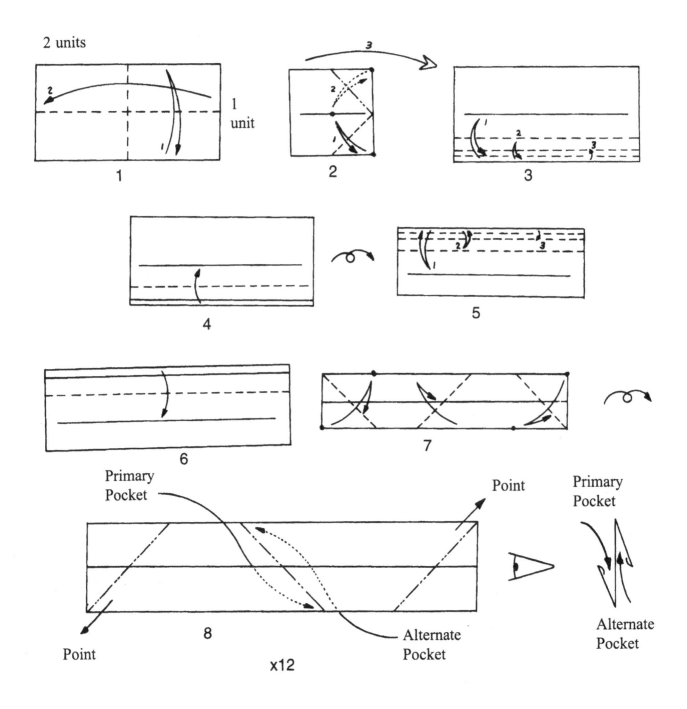

Cube-Corner Stellated Forms
Combining 90 Degrees and 45 Degrees in One Module
by Bennett Arnstein and Rona Gurkewitz

Start with step 10 of the Decoration Box (p. 24). Pictured here is a 6-module Toshie's Jewel shape made from Decoration Box modules by changing the angle at one end of the module to 45 degrees. (The angle at both ends of the Decoration Box module is 90 degrees.) The next page shows how to create other cube-corner stellated forms by changing the angle at one end of the Ninja Star Module and also changing one crease in this module from a mountain to a valley. See the photos on p. 23 and also p. 4.

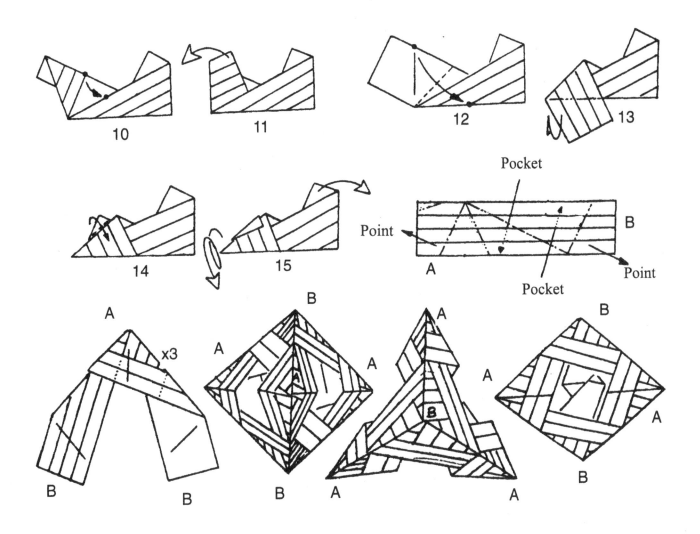

Modified Ninja Star Module
Combining Different Angles in One Module to
Make Cube-Corner Stellated Models

Modification for 6-module Toshie's Jewel. Start with step 6 on p. 32 and make one new crease in the same sense as the original three creases (all valleys). See p. 41.

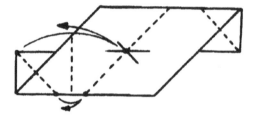

Modification to make other stellated models. Start with step 7 on p. 32 and make one new valley crease. (Note that the original three creases are mountains.) Twenty-four modules make a stellated octahedron and sixty modules make a stellated icosahedron. See the photos on pp. 1, 4, and 23.

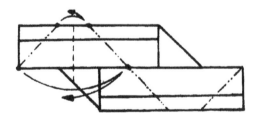

In either case above, the modified end of one module connects to the modified end of another module, and the original end of each module connects to the original end of another module. The points and pockets on the modified module are the same as those on the original module.

60-Degree Half-Square Plank Module

by Bennett Arnstein, Rona Gurkewitz, and Jim Plank

Start with step 5 of LSDB #1, p. 25. This module is a triangle-edge module.

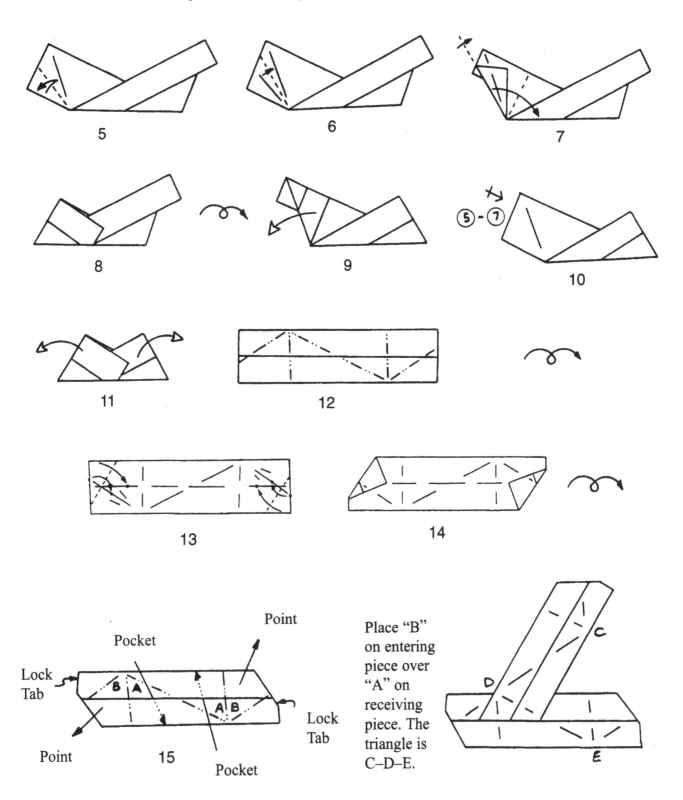

Place "B" on entering piece over "A" on receiving piece. The triangle is C–D–E.

Exact 60-Degree Half-Square Module

by Bennett Arnstein

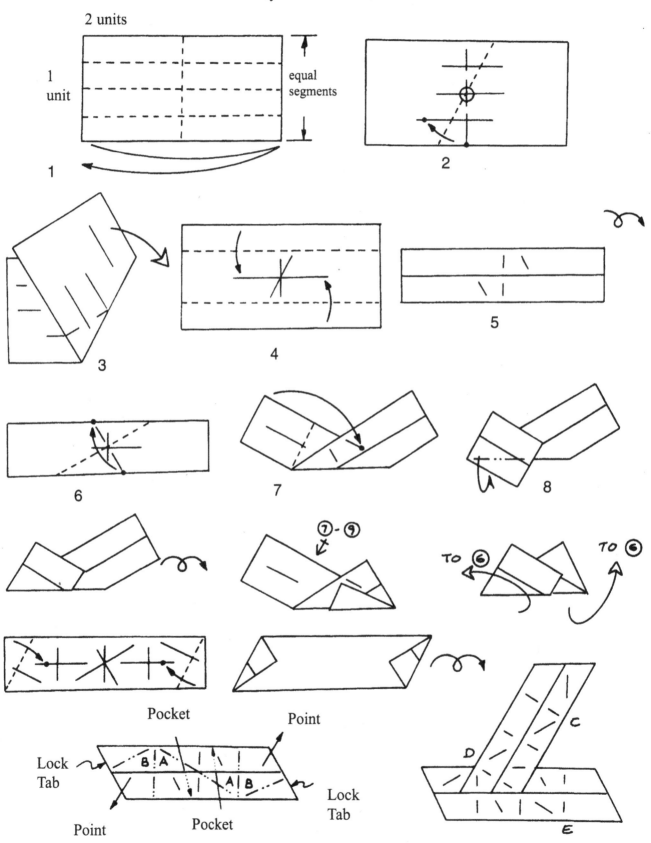

2 units

1 unit

equal segments

1

2

3

4

5

6

7

8

⑦-⑨

TO ⑥   TO ⑥

Pocket

Point

Lock Tab

B A   A B

Point

Pocket

Lock Tab

D   C

E

108-Degree Module
by Lewis Simon
(and independently, Bob Neale)

This is a very sturdy model, a classic. Thirty modules make a
dodecahedron. In step 5, the short crease on the entering
module lines up with the long crease on the receiving module.

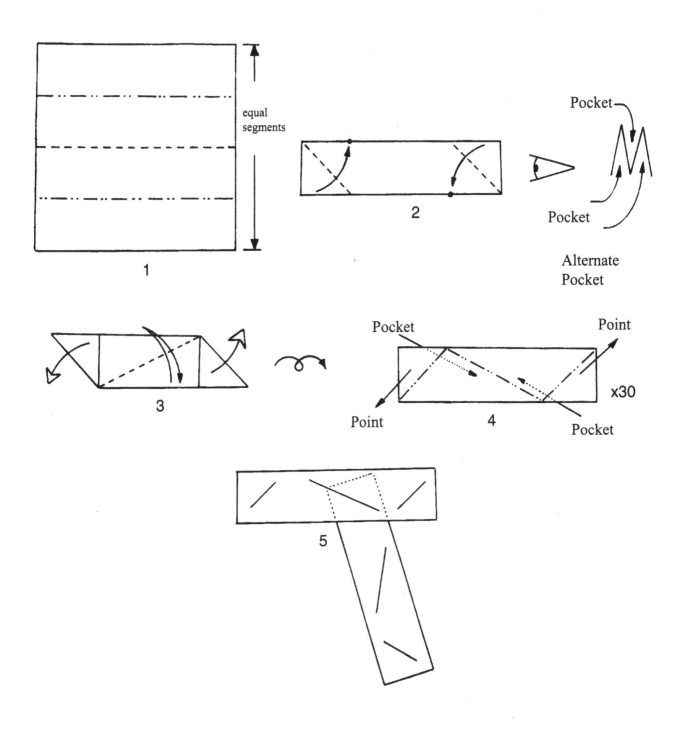

45

Part 5
Gyroscope System

Clockwise: 6-Module Gyroscope from squares
60-Module Rhombicosidodecahedron from Sunkated Gyroscope modules
30-Module Icosidodecahedron from Sunkated Gyroscope modules

Gyroscope
by Lewis Simon

The Gyroscope is an octahedron skeleton with a cube-shaped opening in the center. It is made from six 2-piece modules, with each piece made from a square. Lewis called it a Gyroscope because a small one can be held in one hand, supported on opposite corners, and made to spin by blowing on it. To make one fit outside an existing cube, fold the modules from squares with sides 2.47 times the length of an edge of the cube. A cuboctahedron is made from twelve 2-piece modules and a rhombicuboctahedron is made from twenty-four 2-piece modules.

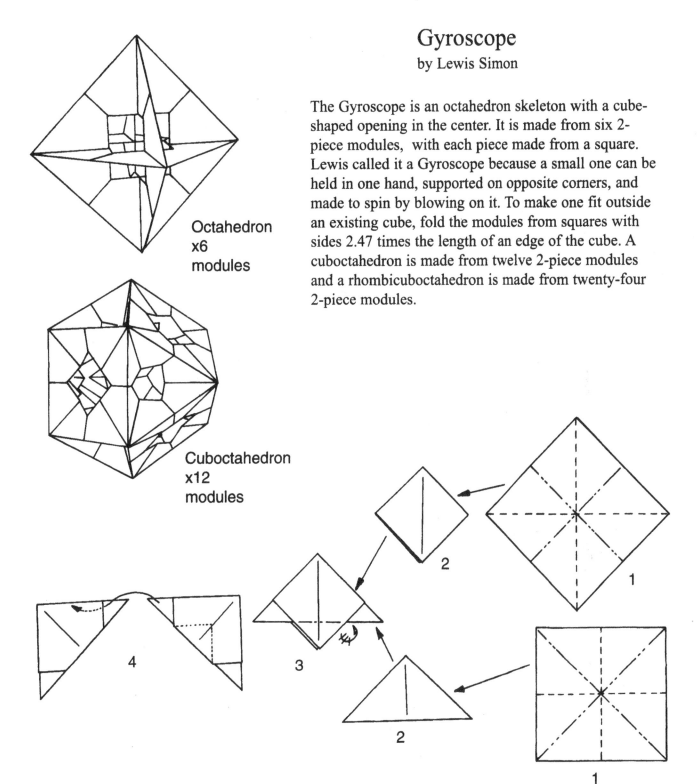

Octahedron
x6
modules

Cuboctahedron
x12
modules

Sunkated Gyroscope Module

by Rona Gurkewitz

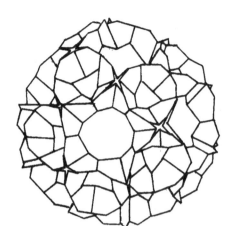

Start with step 4 on p. 47. The polyhedra that can be made from this module are the polyhedra with four edges meeting at every vertex. Some of them are indicated below by the rings (or polygons) that surround a vertex. The sunken vertex of this module corresponds to a vertex of a polyhedron. The resulting polyhedra may be considered truncated.

$$\begin{array}{c|c} 3 & 3 \\ \hline 3 & 3 \end{array}$$ Octahedron: 6 modules, each module is part of four 3-sided rings.

$$\begin{array}{c|c} 3 & 4 \\ \hline 4 & 3 \end{array}$$ Cuboctahedron: 12 modules, each module is part of two 3-sided rings and two 4-sided rings.

$$\begin{array}{c|c} 3 & 4 \\ \hline 4 & 4 \end{array}$$ Rhombicuboctahedron: 24 modules, each module is part of one 3-sided ring and three 4-sided rings.

$$\begin{array}{c|c} 3 & 5 \\ \hline 5 & 3 \end{array}$$ Icosidodecahedron: 30 modules, each module is part of two 3-sided rings and two 5-sided rings. Diagram this page. Photo p. 46.

$$\begin{array}{c|c} 3 & 4 \\ \hline 4 & 5 \end{array}$$ Rhombicosidodecahedron: 60 modules, each module is part of one 3-sided ring, one 5-sided ring, and two 4-sided rings. Photo p. 46.

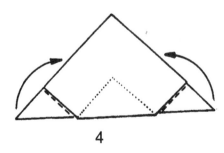

4

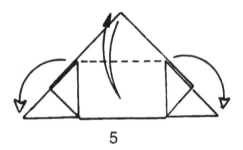

5

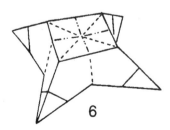

6

7

Triangular Gyroscope

by Lewis Simon

The models in figures A–D are all made from the same module, which is a two-piece module made from two equilateral triangles. This module is the triangular analogue of the original Gyroscope. Both modules consist of a preliminary base (square or triangular) wrapped around and inside a waterbomb base (square or triangular). Many other polyhedral models are possible. For the triangular module, what they have in common is that three edges meet at a point of the model. **A**: Dodecahedron (20), **B**: Hexagonal Prism (12), **C**: Pentagonal Prism (10), **D**: Truncated Tetrahedron (12)

Other possible models include: Truncated Octahedron (24), Buckyball (truncated icosahedron) (60), Egg (truncated hexadecahedron) (48), Hamburger Bun (truncated pentagonal dipyramid) (30), Pickle (truncated triangular dodecahedron (36).

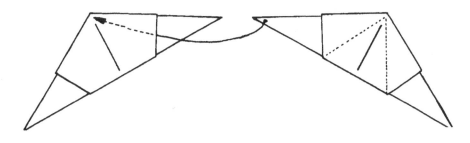

Triangular Gyroscope Assembly

 Truncated tetrahedron: 12 modules. Each module is part of two 6-sided rings and one 3-sided ring. The easiest way to build this is to make four 3-sided rings first. Three 3-sided rings are joined to form a 6-sided ring; then attach the last 3-sided ring.

 Truncated octahedron: 24 modules. Each module is part of two 6-sided rings and one 4-sided ring.

 Dodecahedron: 20 modules. Each module is part of three 5-sided rings.

 Truncated icosahedron (soccer ball): 60 modules. Each module is part of two 6-sided rings and one 5-sided ring.

Poles

Truncated hexadecahedron (egg or potato): 48 modules. 4-sided ring at north pole and south pole. All other rings are either 5-sided or 6-sided. Every module is part of two 6-sided rings and also part of one 3-sided ring at the six polar modules or one 5-sided ring at all other modules between the poles.

Poles

Truncated triangular dodecahedron (pickle or cucumber): 36 modules. 3-sided ring at north pole and south pole. All other rings are either 5-sided or 6-sided. Every module is part of two 6-sided rings and also part of one 3-sided ring at the six polar modules or one 5-sided ring at all other modules between the poles.

Truncated double pentagonal pyramid (hamburger bun): 30 modules. 5-sided ring at north pole and south pole; five 4-sided rings around equator. Every module touches two 6-sided rings.

Poles

Truncated double tetrahedron: 18 modules. 3-sided ring at north pole and south pole; three 4-sided rings around the equator. Every module is part of two 6-sided rings.

Poles

 Pentagon prism: 10 modules. Each module is part of one 5-sided ring and two 4-sided rings.

Hexagon prism: 12 modules. Each module is part of one 6-sided ring and two 4-sided rings.

Part 6
Miscellaneous Modules

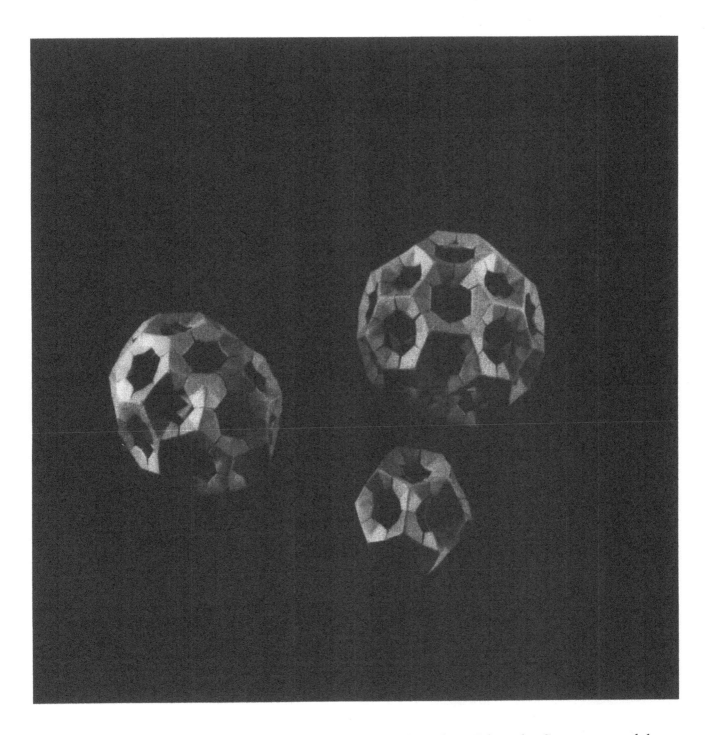

Clockwise: 60-Module Buckyball (truncated icosahedron) from Triangular Gyroscope modules
20-Module Dodecahedron from Triangular Gyroscope modules
48-Module "Egg" (truncated hexadecahedron) from Triangular Gyroscope modules

Twist Cube
by Lewis Simon

Each module forms one face of the cube. To assemble, insert
a point on each module into a pocket of an adjacent module.

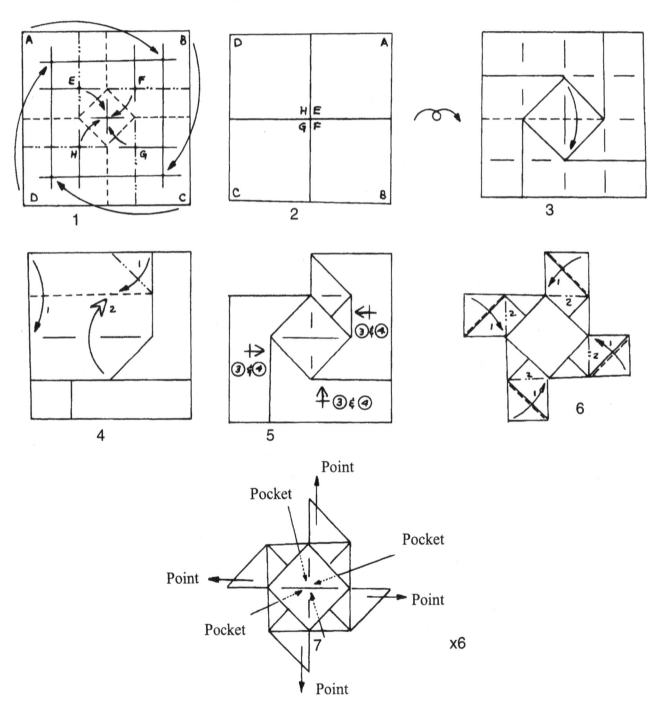

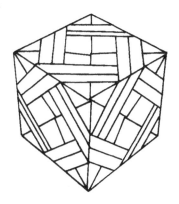

Photo Display Cube
by Lewis Simon

A square photograph may be displayed on each face of the cube by inserting the photograph under the cuffs of the modules. This cube has an interesting pattern formed by the reverse-side colors of the modules.

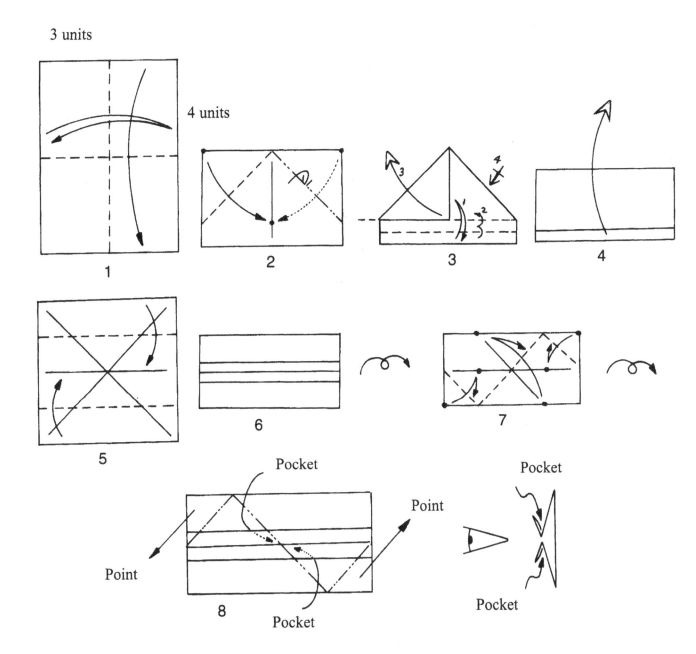

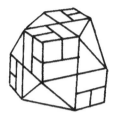

Partially Truncated Modular Cube
by Lewis Simon

This cube has four truncated corners. It is made from 6 modules joined like the 6-module Sonobe cube. Each face of the cube is formed by shape ABCDEF on one module.

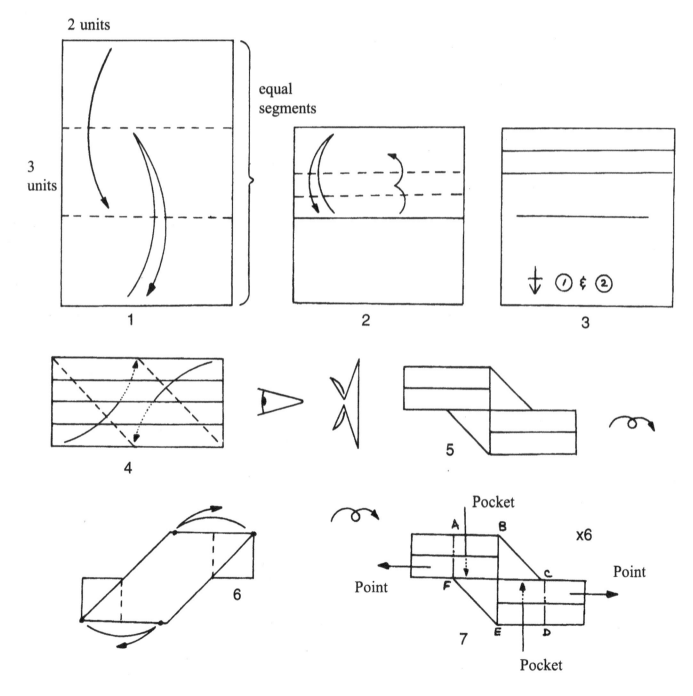

54

Magic Cube #1
by Lewis Simon

Magic Cubes are made from six square sheets of paper. The six squares are folded and joined two at a time to form three strips. Then the three strips are interwoven to form the cube. Step 2: Slip the right sheet inside crease C of the left sheet, and overlap one segment. Fold down the upper third of both sheets along crease B. Step 3: Fold on the existing creases.

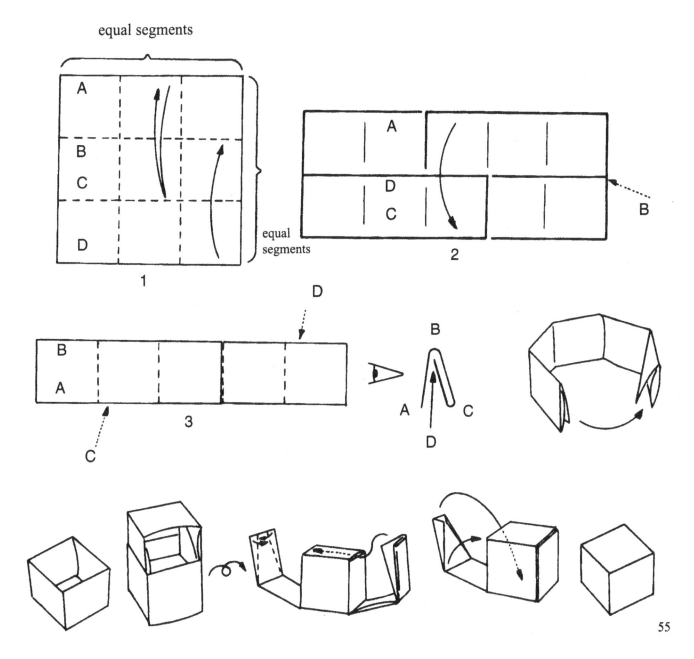

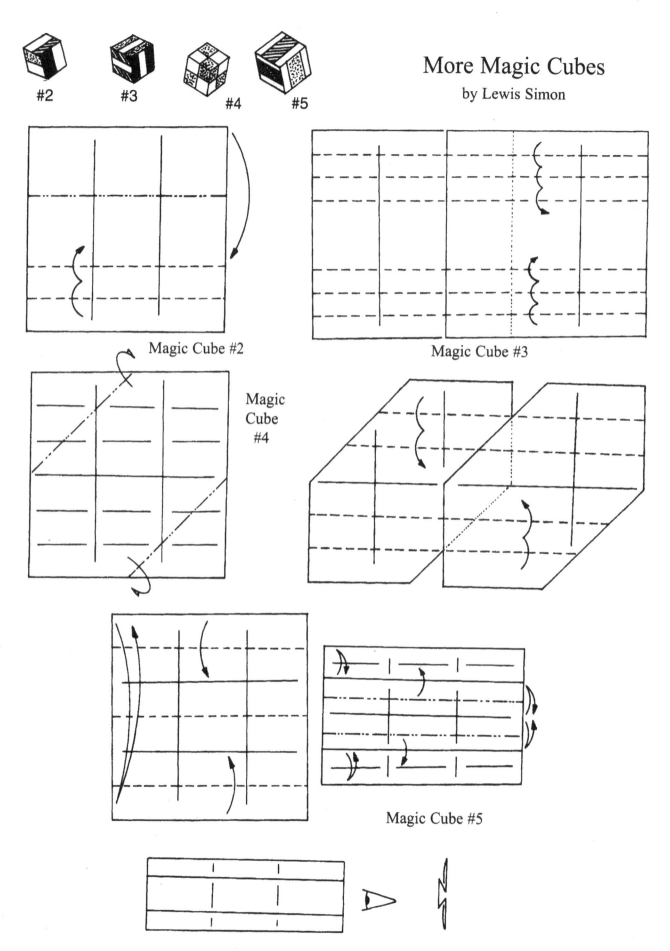

#2　#3　#4　#5

More Magic Cubes
by Lewis Simon

Magic Cube #2

Magic Cube #3

Magic
Cube
#4

Magic Cube #5

#6 #7

More Magic Cubes
by Lewis Simon

Magic Cube #6a exposes the reverse-side color. Each tube is formed from one left module and one right module. Magic Cube #6b is difficult to assemble, as the final joint on the third strip must be connected on the outside of the cube.

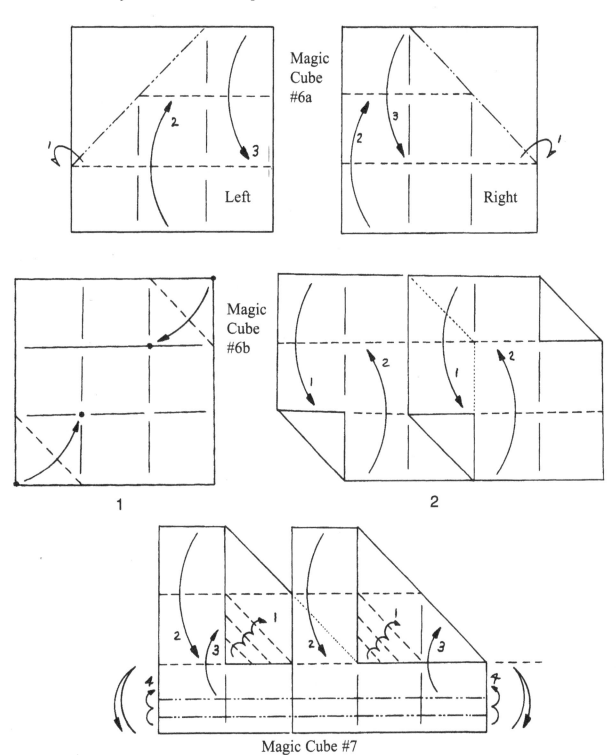

Magic Cube #6a

Left

Right

Magic Cube #6b

1

2

Magic Cube #7

Magic Cube #8

More Magic Cubes
by Lewis Simon

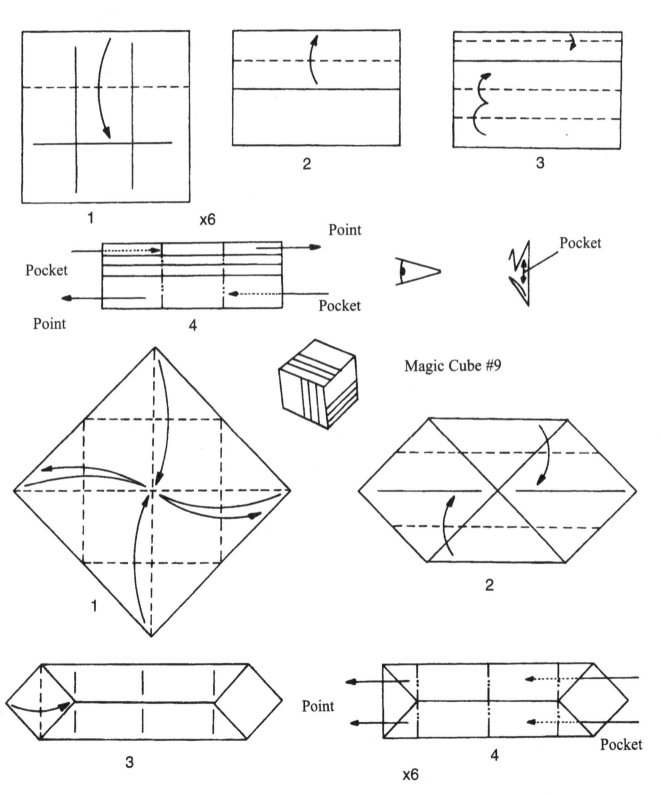

1

x6

2

3

Point

Pocket

Pocket

Point

Pocket

4

Pocket

Magic Cube #9

1

2

3

Point

4

Pocket

x6

Alternate Constructions for Magic Cube #1

by Bennett Arnstein

First alternate construction: Fold three squares by creasing them into four equal segments horizontally and vertically. Cut the squares in half, forming six half-squares. Each half-square is creased into 4 x 2 equal segments. Join two half-squares to form one strip by overlapping two segments at each end. The edge view is shown in figure 1. When forming the tube, make sure that each half-square has one end inside and one end outside the other one. The ends of the third strip fit into the pockets of the second strip as shown in figure 2.

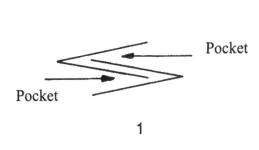

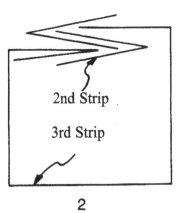

Second alternate construction: Fold two squares into six equal segments horizontally and vertically. Cut the squares in half. Each half-square will be creased into 6 x 3 equal segments. Only three half-squares are used to make one cube. Each half-square is one strip, and is formed into a tube by overlapping two segments at one end into the other end. The edge view is shown in figure 3. The ends of the third strip fit into the pockets of the second strip as shown in figure 4.

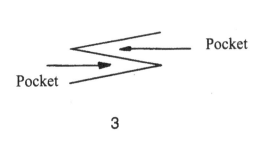

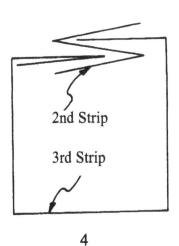